SUMMER
PARTY

THE · CO BLE · STREET · COUSINS

SUMMER
PARTY

CYNTHIA RYLANT

illustrated by

WENDY ANDERSON HALPERIN

Simon & Schuster Books for Young Readers

NEW YORK   LONDON   TORONTO   SYDNEY   SINGAPORE

SIMON & SCHUSTER BOOKS FOR YOUNG READERS
An imprint of Simon & Schuster Children's Publishing Division
1230 Avenue of the Americas
New York, New York 10020

Book design by Heather Wood
The text of this book is set in Garth Graphic.
The illustrations are rendered in pencil and watercolor.
Printed in the United States of America
2   4   6   8   10   9   7   5   3   1

Library of Congress Cataloging-in-Publication Data
Rylant, Cynthia.
Summer Party / by Cynthia Rylant;
illustrated by Wendy Anderson Halperin. —1st ed.
p. cm.—(The Cobble Street cousins; 5)
Summary: Nine-year-old cousins Lily, Rosie, and Tess are sad
when it is time to leave Aunt Lucy, so they plan a party and
get a special surprise to look forward to in the near future.
ISBN 0-689-83241-9
[1. Cousins—Fiction. 2. Aunts—Fiction. 3. Parties—Fiction.]
I. Halperin, Wendy Anderson, ill. II. Title.
PZ7.R982 Su 2001 [Fic]—dc21   00-063538

TABLE OF CONTENTS

To Madison Grace

C.R.

To Joel, Kale, and Lane

W.A.H.

SUMMER
PARTY

A LITTLE WEEPY

𝓘n a pretty blue house on Cobble Street, three girl cousins lived with their wonderful Aunt Lucy. Lily and Rosie were sisters, Tess was their cousin, and they were all nine years old and best friends. They had lived in Aunt Lucy's attic for nearly a year, in wonderful little spaces all their own:

Lily behind long, lacy yellow curtains, with her rabbit collection and her poetry. (Lily wanted to be a writer.) Rosie behind the patch-work quilt, with her rag doll, Angel Girl, and her bear, Henry. And Tess behind the screen painted with palm trees, with her stack of old records (Tess loved to sing) and her cat, Elliott.

The girls loved Aunt Lucy's house and they loved Aunt Lucy and they had had the most wonderful year together. But now their parents—who had been on a world tour with the ballet—were on their way home, and it was time for everything to change.

Lily and Rosie and Tess sat on the front porch swing and talked about it. Or tried to.

"I can't talk about it," said Rosie, her eyes welling up. Of the three cousins, Rosie was the most tender and sentimental.

"I feel like writing a very sad poem," said Lily.

"Or singing a really sad song," said Tess.

The three girls sat quietly, holding hands.
Tess's cat Elliott walked all over their laps,
purring, but it didn't help much.

Suddenly Rosie said, "There's Michael!"

It was Aunt Lucy's boyfriend, Michael, walking down the street. Michael was so nice, and the girls liked him very much. In fact, the cousins were responsible for getting him and Aunt Lucy together. And they loved the fact that even though his family was wealthy, Michael was studying to be a botanist, and he always looked a bit shy and a bit crumpled. The cousins were really hoping he'd be their uncle someday.

Michael walked up onto the porch. He looked at the cousins with a worried smile. "Hi, girls," he said. "Is everything okay?"

And with that, Tess burst into tears and went running into the house. (Tess wanted to be a Broadway actress someday, so she never worried about expressing herself.)

"Goodness!" said Michael. "Something *is* wrong." He sat down on the porch railing and looked at Rosie, who seemed nearly ready to burst into tears herself. "What is it, Rosie?" Michael asked. "Can I help?"

Rosie shook her head. "It's just that we have to go home soon," she said in a quiet voice. "Our real homes."

"And Rosie and I will miss Tess *so much!*" added Lily. "And Elliott and Aunt Lucy and this wonderful old house and . . . and . . . *everything.*"

Rosie nodded. "And you, too," she told Michael.

Michael was quiet a moment. Then he said, "You're right. It *is* sad. No one likes to leave people and places they love, even if there are more people and places *ahead* of them to love."

Rosie and Lily nodded. The screen door opened, and Tess came outside carrying a box of tissues. "I'm okay now," she said with a sniffle. "I just needed to let go."

Michael smiled.

Tess sat down on the swing again and took Lily's hand. "At least you and Rosie have each other," she told Lily. "I won't have anybody."

"You'll have Elliott," said Lily.

"Oh," said Tess. "You're right. I do love Elliott."

Elliott was back in her lap, purring.

The three cousins looked as if they *all* might burst into tears and *all* run into the house together. So Michael said, "Why don't we go somewhere fun? We'll stop at the flower shop and tell your Aunt Lucy where we're going. Then we'll do something fun."

The girls didn't speak.

"No one wants fun?" asked Michael.

Rosie gave a little grin.

"I guess I'll have to take Elliott instead," said Michael.

Tess and Lily both smiled.

"Can we go to a movie?" asked Rosie. "A funny movie?"

Tess and Lily nodded in agreement.

"The funniest movie in town," said Michael. "My treat. Plus all the popcorn and candy you can eat."

"Yay!" said Tess.

Everyone looked at her in surprise.

"Oops," she said, covering her mouth. "I forgot to be sad."

Everyone laughed. It was so good to be feeling better.

H O P E !

After the movie—which was about a silly monkey who made them laugh and laugh—the cousins and Michael went back to Aunt Lucy's flower shop. They walked past the beautiful flowers and the window box and the bright blue bench out in front. Michael opened the door: *ding!*

"I love this shop so much," said Rosie.

"Me too," said Tess and Lily.

13

They all felt a little weepy again.

But there was Aunt Lucy, with hugs for everyone and offers of tea and cookies, and the cousins couldn't feel weepy for long.

Over tea, they talked about their parents' homecoming.

"It isn't that we don't love them," said Tess.

"Or don't miss them," said Rosie.

"Or don't want to see them," added Lily.

Aunt Lucy nodded sympathetically.

"It's just that we don't want to miss each other," said Lily. "And you."

Aunt Lucy smiled. "It *is* hard," she said quietly. And for a moment the cousins thought *she* was going to cry.

And they all realized something: Aunt Lucy was sad, too!

Somehow that made them feel better.

"But we all have to be brave and full of hope," said Aunt Lucy. "We have to make plans for the *future,* don't you think? Really fun plans."

Lily, Rosie, and Tess all looked at each other. They almost felt a little brave. They almost felt some hope.

"Let's make plans!" said Tess. "Really good
ones!"

"Okay!" said Rosie and Lily.

"So—what would make you girls happy?"
asked Michael. "What could you look
forward to?"

"Well . . . ," said Tess, thinking. "How about
reunions?"

"Definitely!" cried Lily.

"*Family* reunions," said Rosie. "For *this* family, us and you two."

"Sounds perfect," said Aunt Lucy. "When?"

The cousins thought.

"How about every single summer until we're all grown up?" asked Rosie.

"Yes!" said Tess.

"Definitely!" said Lily.

Aunt Lucy smiled. "You are welcome here anytime at all," she said. "You could come and stay all summer long, in your very same beds in the attic, if you wanted to."

"*All summer long?*" asked Rosie.

"Yay!" cheered the cousins.

"Pretty good plans so far," said Michael, smiling and pouring himself another cup of tea.

"What about something fun for now?" asked Aunt Lucy. "Would you like to do something special when your parents arrive?"

The cousins looked at each other.

"I have an idea," said Lily, who was always good at ideas. "Let's have a summer party for them. Like those pretty ones in the movies, with Japanese lanterns on the lawn and fancy punch and—"

"Entertainment," finished Tess. "We're *really* good at that."

"Maybe I could make little vegetable people," said Rosie.

"Little what?" asked Tess.

"Little vegetable people," said Rosie. "You know."

Everyone looked at Rosie with blank faces.

Then Lily laughed and hugged her sister. "Rosie, you're the best," said Lily.

"You mean like a little broccoli mailman?" asked Tess.

Rosie smiled.

It was good to have plans.

PARTY PLANS

That evening the cousins gathered in the middle of the attic (they called it The Playground) with their dolls and bears and rabbit and one real cat to talk about their summer party.

"I wish we could have an ice sculpture," said Lily, changing the jacket on one of her rabbits. "Fancy parties always have ice sculptures."

"We could make pretty ice cubes at least," said Rosie. "Red and blue and green ones. It's easy with food coloring."

"We could serve pink lemonade with colored ice!" said Tess. "Great!"

Lily wrote down that plan for the party. "What about food?" she asked. (Rosie had given up on the vegetable people idea. She worried they might wilt.)

"We could use Aunt Lucy's cookie cutters to make pretty sandwiches," said Rosie. "Kitty sandwiches and teapot sandwiches and umbrella sandwiches. Aunt Lucy has good cookie cutters."

"Great!" said Tess. "Rosie, you are really good at this." (Tess wasn't really surprised. Rosie was always the best at making things pretty or cozy. Rosie was very domestic.)

"Let's make lemon cookies," said Lily. "I love lemon cookies."

"Me too," said Rosie.

"Can we also have fudge—for me?" asked Tess.

"Fudge for Tess," said Lily, writing it down.

"What about entertainment?" asked Rosie.

"My favorite subject," said Tess.

"We should choose a theme," said Lily.

"How about 'good-byes'?" asked Tess.

"Oh no," Rosie said. "We'd all be blubbery and weepy."

"*That's* entertainment!" Tess said with a grin.

"How about 'forever'?" asked Lily. "We'll be cousins forever and friends forever and we'll love this wonderful old house forever."

"Don't forget Elliott," said Rosie with a giggle, scratching the kitty's head.

"Sure," said Tess. "There are lots of good songs about forever."

"Good poems, too," said Lily.

"*You* should write one," said Rosie. "Your poems are best."

Lily smiled. "Thanks."

"I just got a *great* idea!" said Tess.

"What?" asked Lily.

"Let's have fortunes for everybody! We can write them down and then roll them into little packages, and everybody will get one. You know how Aunt Lucy said it's all about the *future* now."

"Perfect!" cried Lily and Rosie.

Tess grinned. "I am so brilliant," she said.

The cousins' summer party was really beginning.

28

HAPPY FAMILIES

One week later poems had been written (and rewritten), songs had been sung (and sung again), and cookie cutters had been chosen (that was the easy part). The summer party was nearly at hand.

But first the cousins had to meet their parents at the airport. Aunt Lucy and Michael drove them.

"Why am I so jittery?" asked Tess.

"Too much caffeine?" asked Rosie with a grin.

"It's only my mom," said Tess. "I shouldn't be nervous."

"I'm jittery, too," said Lily.

"It's normal to be nervous," said Aunt Lucy. "It means you're looking forward to seeing them."

"I wonder if Mom and Dad are nervous, too?" asked Rosie. "Do you think so, Lily?"

"I don't know," said Lily. "After so many years onstage, you'd think nothing would make them nervous."

"Bridges make me nervous," said Michael.

"Really?" asked Tess.

"Yes. I usually shut my eyes going over them," answered Michael.

"Wow," said Tess. "I'm glad you're not driving!"

Michael looked at Aunt Lucy and smiled.

At the airport they all found the gate where their parents' jet would be landing.

"Do I look all right?" Rosie asked Michael.

"Like a Rose," he said.

Rosie grinned. Michael was so nice.

Then finally Lily and Rosie's parents and Tess's mother were all there.

Tess's mother dropped her bags and gave Tess a big squeeze. "Tess, *look*

at you!" she said. "How *pretty* you are! How you've grown. Oh, I adore your hat!"

Tess grinned from ear to ear. It was the same sweet mom.

Rosie and Lily ran back and forth hugging
each parent. Rosie couldn't stop giggling. And
Lily giggled because Rosie did.

"Look at these giggle-girls!" said their
father.

"We missed you so much," said their
mother.

Aunt Lucy and Michael held hands and
watched.

Somehow, even with all the excitement and hugs and giggles, everyone made it smoothly back to Aunt Lucy's house. (Tess and her mother took a taxi so they could fit all the extra bags in.)

At home the cousins sat around the big table in Aunt Lucy's kitchen and talked and laughed with their *much larger* family for hours. The cousins had forgotten how happy their parents made them, how much fun they could be. The parents told stories of the things they'd seen all over the world.

"I can't wait to travel the world," said Lily.

"Me too," said Tess.

"I'll pick you up at the airport," Rosie said.

Everybody laughed, and Aunt Lucy gave
Rosie a hug. "I'm not sure I want to give
these beautiful girls back," Aunt
Lucy said.

"You mean we have to take them back?"
asked Tess's mom.

Everyone laughed again. The wonderful
blue house with red geraniums was full of
happiness once more.

FRIENDS AND FORTUNES

The next evening was the summer party. Lily practiced her poem all afternoon while she made little sandwiches. Tess practiced her song while she colored the ice. And Michael and Rosie sat on the front porch, writing fortunes and rolling them into little ribboned packages.

"Let's make them funny," said Rosie with a giggle.

"Okay," said Michael.

"And we shouldn't tell each other what we're writing," said Rosie. "If I get one of yours, I want to be surprised."

"Likewise," said Michael. "How do you spell 'ophthalmologist'?"

Rosie stared at him for a second.

Then they both burst into laughter.

Rosie felt so happy. So full of hope. Everything would be all right.

At the end of the day, Aunt Lucy and Michael strung Japanese lanterns through the trees in Aunt Lucy's courtyard. The cousins set up five little tables covered with pretty red cloths and flowered napkins. The tables were strewn with sparkling glitter and confetti, and a pretty candle glowed in the center of each.

"Really nice!" said Rosie.

"Aren't you glad I thought of the sparkles?" asked Tess.

"Yes!" said Rosie.

The cousins then wrote out place cards for each table so the guests would all know where to sit. The place cards were shaped like cats, in honor of Elliott (who had not been invited because he wouldn't keep off the glitter).

Then Michael put a small festive package bearing a fortune on each plate.

"Beautiful!" said Lily.

At seven o'clock the guests all arrived. There were the parents, of course. Plus Mr. French and Mrs. White, dear neighbors of the cousins, and Mrs. White's friend, Senator Harrison. Michael's father was out of town, but Michael did manage to borrow Yardley, his father's basset hound. The cousins were delighted to see Yardley again.

When everyone was seated, they all had delicious tiny sandwiches in wonderful shapes (even giraffes!) and lemon cookies and chocolate fudge and a very colorful punch that Tess called the Cousins' Crayon Concoction. The guests loved it.

After eating, everyone settled down for entertainment. First, Tess sang a beautiful song called "Friends Forever," which nearly had Rosie a blubbery mess, but she managed to hold up.

Then Lily read her poem:

Cousins

On Cobble Street there once were three
Cousins living happily.
One with patchwork, one with lace,
One who sang in every place.
They baked cookies, they made tea,
They sewed very daintily.
Cousins in the morning light,
Cousins there to say good night.
In my heart there'll always be
A big blue house with cousins three.

That did make Rosie cry. And nearly everyone else. The cousins got lots of hugs from everyone.

Then Rosie remembered:

"Don't forget your fortunes, everybody!"

Suddenly it was a party again, with all the guests laughing and saying funny things. Tess missed Elliott so much, she had to run up to the attic to give him a kiss. "Don't open the fortunes until I get back, please!" she said. She ran quickly and was back in minutes.

"Okay!" said Aunt Lucy. "Let's open our fortunes!"

There was a great flurry of unwrapping and untangling and silent readings. Then *much* laughter!

"Mine says, 'An ophthalmologist has eyes for you,'" said Mr. French. He laughed and laughed.

"Mine says, 'You will inherit a freezer because you are so cool,'" said Tess's mother.

"I'm going to be a belly dancer in New Hampshire," said Lily and Rosie's father.

Everyone read their funny fortunes aloud for all to hear. Everyone except Aunt Lucy. She had been very quiet.

"What does yours say, Aunt Lucy?" asked Tess.

"Yes, what does yours say?" asked Lily.

Aunt Lucy was very pale. She looked across the tables at Michael, who had knelt down to pet Yardley.

Michael rose up and took a deep breath. Then the cousins watched as he walked over to stand before their Aunt Lucy.

"What does yours say, Lucy?" Michael asked softly.

Rosie's eyes were wide as saucers. Lily held still.

Tess barely breathed. Something was *happening*.

"It says, 'Will you marry me?'" whispered Aunt Lucy.

The cousins gasped.

"Will you?" asked Michael. "I thought if I asked you here in front of the cousins, you couldn't say no." He smiled shyly.

Aunt Lucy smiled back at him and took his hand. "Yes, Michael," she said. "I would love to marry you."

"EEEEEEEEK!" The cousins couldn't help themselves! They *had* to scream, they were so happy!

The girls ran over and jumped up and down and hugged Michael and Aunt Lucy again and again. All the guests applauded and cheered and declared their well-wishes. Even Yardley howled! It was a true celebration.

Later that night, curled up cozy under several quilts in The Playground, the cousins talked of everything that had happened and everything that was *going* to happen.

"Aunt Lucy was right," said Tess. "Be brave. Have hope. Make plans for the *future!*"

"I can't believe there are wedding plans!"
said Lily.

"I think an August wedding will be perfect,"
said Rosie. "Everything's in bloom."

"*And* we get to come back in two months!"
said Tess.

The girls squealed with delight and snuggled
closer.

"Isn't it amazing how we were so sad and now we're so happy?" asked Lily.

"And green," said Rosie.

"*Green*?" repeated Lily and Tess.

Rosie held up her fingers. They were all green. "I spilled the food coloring when I was cleaning up," she said. "And it's not easy being—"

"Don't tell us!" cried Tess.

The cousins giggled and giggled.

There was *so* much to look forward to!

0.5 Points
3.5 RL

/